This journal is meant to be given from a parent to their child. Each day since my son was born, I have written him a note, and in this Journal, you will find some of my favorites. By writing a note to your child, you will be giving them a priceless gift. Take it from me; I was raised by a single mother who passed away when I was just a kid. I would have done anything to know more about her and what her thoughts were on life. This Journal will give your child the opportunity to know what yours are. I hope this Journal, when completed, gives you both peace of mind and everlasting memories.
-Tommy Feight

To: _______________

From: _______________

You will not always be happy
with me, but I will always love
you. No matter what.

You may not always have all
you want, but you should
always appreciate all you have.

nowledge is power; read as
much as you can.

You know you are in love when you
can't sleep because reality is better
than your dreams.
-DR. Seuss

Believe in yourself. You can do anything you put your mind to.

You can pick your friends and
you can pick your nose, but
you can't pick your friends
nose.

Iy favorite things in life don't cost
oney; it's really clear that the most
precious resource is time.
-Steve Jobs

Always be polite. Say
please and thank you.

Do your best.

Life's most persistent and urgent question
is, "what are you doing for others?"
-MLK

you have your health, you have
verything, so stay active and eat
your vegetables.

Be competitive and strive to be
the best at everything you do.

ou were given two ears and one
mouth because sometimes it's
better to listen than to speak.

When you shake someone's hand,
always look them in the eye.

Be a leader not a follower.

History remembers who won.
Not *who* came in second.

Stand up for yourself.
Never allow yourself you
be bullied.

If you commit to something, see
it through to the end. Don't get
in the habit of quitting because
bad habits are hard to break.

Hopes high, head down low.
You can accomplish anything, you
just have to be willing to put in the
work to get there.

Death is a part of life. The worst part.
So tell the ones you love how much they
mean to you as often as possible.

You will always be my
greatest accomplishment.

We all make mistakes, learn
from them and be
accountable.

Be yourself; true happiness
omes when you can be open
nd free about the person you
are.

Be generous; give to others
not for them but for you.

Don't put off for tomorrow
what could be done today.
Do it now!

Make your bed every day. It sets the tone
for the day. Once you complete one task,
you can complete anything else that comes
your way that day.

Integrity is doing the
right thing when no one
else is watching.
-C.S. Lewis

Even when I am not
there to hold your hand,
know that I will always
have your back.

Bush your teeth, floss,
wash your hands and take
regular showers.

Your *word* is your bond.
Don't break it for
anyone.

Learn to cook. It will do
you a world of good to
know how to feed yourself
and others.

If you set your goals ridiculously
high and it's a failure, you will fail
above everyone else's successes.
-James Cameron

Respect your elders; with
  age comes wisdom.

Say no to drugs.

Some decisions you
make can affect your
whole life; choose wisely.

Try to walk in someone
else's shoes before you tell
them how to wear them.

Hard work beats talent when
talent doesn't work hard.
-Tim Notke

Everyone makes mistakes.
You have to own them and
accept responsibility so that
you can learn from them
and move on.

emember, no matter what happened
yesterday, or today; you still have
your whole life in front of you.

I've failed over and over and over
again. That's why I succeed.
    -Michael Jordan

Be grateful and always
show gratitude.

You can be anything you want in life,
believe in yourself, and work hard, and
you will put yourself in a position for
all your dreams to come true.

An investment in knowledge
pays the best interest.
-Benjamin Franklin

Read, Read, Read!
It will take you places
you never imagined.

Be a good teammate not
just in sports but in life.

Every day in every way,
I'm getting better and
better.
-Emile Coue

Cheaters never win, and
winners never cheat.

Winners never quit, and
quitters never win

he life you want you can have,
prepare yourself for it by
reading all you can about it.

It's the thought that counts.

He *who* has overcome his
fears *will* truly be free.
-Aristotle

You can be anything you
want in life, just believe it, and
you can achieve it.

you give more of yourself,
you will get back more in
return.

Good habits are the key to
success; bad habits are the
unlocked door to failure.
-Og Mandino

You must fail first before you
succeed, so if you never
accept failure, you will
always succeed.

If you want to make more
money, always start with how
you can help more people.

I am your biggest fan.

Pick friends that lift you up,
not ones that put you down.

Drink lots of water,
it's your filtration
system, and it will
keep you healthy.

Keep your commitments. Do what you
say you are going to do. Dependability
is a sign of good character.

t's better to give than to
receive.

Birds of a feather flock
together, be sure to pick
the right birds to fly with.

Whatever you think and
elieve, you can achieve with a
positive mental attitude.

When you have a problem,
look for solutions, not who
to blame.

Be humble; let the results
speak for themselves.

Start a business early.
Learn how money works.

Good character is doing
the right thing when
nobody is watching.

Pay attention to what you
post online. The internet is
written in pen and
remembers everything.

Stand up for yourself. If you know
in your heart and in your mind
that you are right, don't back
down from anyone or anything!

The surest way to command
the respect of others is by
respecting yourself first.

You have to be different
  to make a difference.

A good leader is one who shares
the credit for all success and
assumes responsibility for all
failures.

Have higher expectations for
ourself than others have for you.

Don't overthink things once
you have a plan take action.

One reason people don't recognize
opportunity when it comes along is it
is often dressed in overalls and looks
like work.
-Thomas Edison

Procrastination is the bad habit of
putting off something for tomorrow
that should have been done yesterday.
DO IT NOW!

Put 10% of every dollar
you earn in investing into
something for your future.

When things are not
going well, remember
that this too shall pass.

At the end of the day, the
only person who will ever be
responsible for your actions
is you.

You have to give before
you get.

It's better to imitate a
successful person than to
be jealous of them.

Don't be a gossip.

Be positive; look for the
rainbows, not for the rain.

When you set goals for yourself,
make sure they are based on
doing the right thing.

Successful people are
optimistic people.

What other people think of
you is none of your business.
-Eleanor Roosevelt

The first way to have a
healthy mind is to have a
healthy body.

A goal without a plan to
achieve it is just a wish.

Give someone a pat on
the back when they
deserve it.

Small minds think about
things. Great minds
think about ideas.

Don't be afraid of failure,
    be afraid of regret.

You will be wealthy when
your assets bring in more
than your liabilities.

Emulate and try to follow in the
footsteps of people who have
already accomplished your dreams.
They will show you the path.

There is no substitute for
hard *work*.

he world makes room, stands aside,
d gets out of the way of the person
who knows where they are going.

Luck is the residue of design. You would be
surprised how lucky you can be when you are
ready and prepared to take advantage of
opportunities.

Be confident and
believe in yourself.
YOU CAN DO IT!

Learn to visualize the
things you want. You have
to see it to believe it.

's not about how hard you hit; it's about
how hard you can get hit and keep
moving forward, how much you can take
and keep moving forward; that's how
winning is done.
-Rocky Balboa

Spending time with you is
the best part of my day.

Fall down seven
get up eight.

Read books. They will open
doors for you that you did
not even realize were closed.

A *winning* team is one *where*
everyone recognizes that *when*
one member is successful, the
whole team *wins.*

Do good and put good out in
the world, and it will return
to you.

will do anything to protect
you and keep you safe.

Create your buzz, and the
bees *will* follow.

e reason it's lonely at the top is
because most people won't do
hat's necessary to get up there.

Failure to plan is planning to fail.
-John Wooden

Don't eat yellow snow.

The only way you will ever
know is to try.

Spend time each day in
thought. Your mind is a
muscle. To strengthen it, you
have to exercise.

The universe listens, talk to it,
but when you do speak
clearly.

When life speeds up on you, and
you want to slow it down, take
a deep breath and count to ten.

Win or lose, always be a
good sport nobody likes a
sore loser.

You would be surprised by how
little bad luck you have when
you are a positive person.

When you make a mess, you have to clean it up.

Don't follow the crowd.
Let the crowd follow you.
        -Margret Thatcher

Average anything will never
get you extraordinary
results.

The best things come to those
who go out and get them.

In life, when you are in charge,
the buck stops with you.

Don't compromise on your
wants and needs; just find
ways to accomplish them.

Knowledge is power, so to
become invincible, you need
to keep learning.

Whenever you are at your
lowest, remember that
someone out there has it
worse.

Not every shot you take will
make it, but they will all be
worth it.

A person who won't read has
no advantage over one who
cant read.
-Mark Twain

Focus on the possibilities for
success, not the potential for
failure.

Find something you love to
do and go after it with
everything you have.

The six best doctors you can have
are sunlight, rest, exercise, diet,
self-confidence, and friends.
-Steve Jobs

You can if you believe you can.

Be grateful for all
you have.

aking a regular impact of doing and
embracing uncomfortable things will
have a positive impact on your life.

When I give you a hard time,
it's only so you can reap the
benefits later.

Your time is your greatest asset and
currency, invest and spend it wisely.

It's impossible to think negative
thoughts in a positive way.

ook for mentors. Nobody will be a better
ide to get you where you want to go than
somebody who has already been there.

When all else fails,
go with your gut.

If you think about problems, you will find problems. If you think about solutions, you will find solutions.

The person who makes it is the
person who keeps going after
everyone else has quit.

Your life will never change
unless YOU make changes. The
answers always start with you.

Keep your hands to yourself.

Don't make excuses; once
you start making them,
you never stop.

Discipline is doing things
you hate doing but doing
them like you love them.
-Mike Tyson

If you surround yourself with five
millionaires you will be the 6th.
If you surround yourself with five
idiots you will be the 6th.
Your friends can either lift you up or
hold you down, choose wisely.

You are the beat of my
heart.

Have a list of goals and keep them
somewhere that you can see them, and then
take steps every day to reach them. Inch by
inch, it's a synch; yard by yard is hard.

Don't stop working until your
signature becomes an autograph.

Doubt is the killer of success,
do not let doubt creep in.
Believe in yourself.

No one can upset you or
make you angry unless you
let them.

Attack your faults and water your virtues

Failure happens to everyone; how you deal with failure defines your character.

There is a major difference between
an acquaintance and a friend, don't
treat them the same.

Don't ask other people to do
anything you would not do
yourself.

Be brave.
Your heart will always lead you in the
right direction if you are courageous
enough to listen to it.

Do what you love and you will
always love what you do.

your mission in life is to make everyone
like you, you are going to fail, so it's
better to make everyone respect you.

If at first you don't succeed,
then try try again.

Don't be a sore loser. If
you don't like losing
that bad, then *win*.

Nothing in life is worse
than wasted talent.

No problem is new.
Someone else has been
through it before, so don't
be afraid to ask for advise.

Try to be a rainbow in someone
else's cloud.
-Maya Angelou

Positive action creates
positive results.

Remember, there are no shortcuts in life.
Trust me; I have looked.

Worrying is like a rocking chair;
it keeps you busy, but it doesn't
get you anywhere.
-Will Rogers

It's always darkest
before the dawn.

Watching you grow has been
the highlight of my life.

When opportunity knocks,
answer the door.

Actions speak louder than words.
Don't talk about it. Be about it.

Don't settle for less than
what you deserve.

If you believe you can.
You can!

Be a leader, not
a follower.

You are the average of
your five closest friends;
choose wisely.

Be nice.
It costs you nothing, but it pays
handsomely.

If it were easy, everyone
would do it.

If you are only willing to do
what is easy, life will be hard,
but if you are willing to do
what is hard, life will be easy.

If you are grateful for all you
have, then you will always
have all you need.

Early to bed, early to rise
makes a man healthy and wise.
-Benjamin Franklin

You inspire me to be the best version
of me I can be.
Thank You!